InnerSessions

InnerSessions
Poems

by

Linda Drajem
Barbara Q. Faust
Kathy Shoemaker

Aventine Press

Published by Aventine Press
1023 4th Ave #204
San Diego CA, 92101
www.aventinepress.com

ISBN: 1-59330-502-8

Printed in the United States of America

Acknowledgements

We wish to thank most especially our mentor and guide, Jimmie Margaret Gilliam. Her generosity illuminates these pages. Marj Norris inspired us to begin this journey. We thank Bob Drajem, Keith Elkins and Linda Lavid for their time and effort. We thank our photographer, Sally Johnson, for her gift of revealing the beauty hidden in the natural world. As always, our gratitude goes to the poets who are the Women of the Crooked Circle.

INTRODUCTION

In the fall of 1991 I offered a master class, "The Translation of Silence", sponsored by Just Buffalo Literary Center; eighteen women gathered in downtown Buffalo, New York at the Calumet Café on Chippewa Street. Unknown to any of us, we were part of a historic moment that would open to a community of women writers, The Women of the Crooked Circle.

Linda Drajem, Barbara Faust and Kathy Shoemaker are an integral part of this band of sisters. Their poetry originates both from the work of the poet *in solitude*, a solo springhead, and from the act of poets *in relationship,* the communal river. These poems explore recessed gardens and secret wounds. They go inward to places where the poet becomes Muse to herself - where with her own hands she forces Censorship's sealed door - where through her imagination the voiceless other may share.

In *InnerSessions,* this trio of poets takes us to the *edge* of silence.

jimmie margaret gilliam

Preface

We did not expect that this adventure would result in the weaving of our lives into the book you hold in your hands. In the beginning we met, gathered our poems, set deadlines, changed deadlines, revised, and winnowed. We made friends with our computers. We did not expect to create this place where our poems live together and speak to each other as well as stand alone. We bring you our poems. They are our footprints on the wider world equal to our living in it.

Table of Contents

Echoes

Linda Drajem

barbara q. faust

Kathy Shoemaker

ECHOES

Women and Writing

Neon I
Kathy Shoemaker

The homeopathist told me, "*This remedy Neon will help you with your relationships.*" Round white pills that taste like air and come in a tiny brown bottle? Neon should be nebulous, bright green, float dreamily inside flexible glass tubes hanging from store fronts to advertise haircuts, age-erasing creams, sun-tanning booths, sports bars – all one could ever want in a green serpentine sign. The homeopathist told me, "*Dissolve the pills under your tongue. Don't use caffeine or strong mints. Come back to talk to me in three months. It may work or it may not. You might need a different remedy.*"

I took it and my son called to wish me happy birthday on Mother's Day.

Neon II
Kathy Shoemaker

I made a date with my breath
Took another dose of Neon
Dissolved all the words in my mind

I saw them pack up just before I arrived
They carried old and weathered luggage
Packed and unpacked
(I think they lived here a long time
And will return if I dare to turn away)

They look back surreptitiously as they leave
Hoping to remain invisible.
Found the place where words have moved away
Left behind no belongings
No fuzzy winter mittens or scarves
No baseball caps with logos
No black spaghetti strap dresses
No sensible brown skirts, sneakers, sandals or high heels
No socks or empty wrappers from power bars.

I don't know why they didn't stay
It's such a lovely place—I've been here before
Squatting in the bank of woodland creek
Peering into the dark water where the frogs live
Waiting uncounted moments for them to emerge
Until unafraid we sit together.
Afternoon shadows stretch like soft sheets
Over thick beds of pine needles
Invite me to lie down and watch the clouds
Come and go on their strange journeys
It doesn't matter where they are going.

The stream is friendly— neither too wide nor too swift
Speaks to me without words
Tells me where the brown trout lie in wait
For newly hatched nymphs
Where to wait for the water snake
To cross to the other side
Where to find the ferns unfolding like green origami
By mid-summer they will be high enough for me
To tunnel through with rabbits.
"If you go far enough, the stream tells me,
You will come to a small waterfall
Speaking another dialect."

the shawl
(for n)
barbara q. faust

late in the afternoons
walking within the dove gray wash of the Himalayas
we women come
gather moments from our lives
bits of bright turquoise   coral
the scarlet of our celebrations
silken calligraphy cast upon a floor within each dusk
before the sun lays her face behind the mountains

we collect the ruby the golden the bronze
carry threads away in our arms
sit together in our homes upon earthen floors
and look up into the ceiling of the world
where the sun lives with the moon
we braid incarnadine   saffron   forest green
far above the tree line
connect all these miles of other womens' lives
their smallest moments—
part of an exhalation a kiss from just the upper lip
the last of a sigh—
we spin these together
thread them between the breasts of mountains
cast them across the charmeuse skin of oceans
a glow on the shoulders of a sister we will never see
who wears our stories like a gift

you can open the door
(for the poets)
barbara q. faust

once in a park on an ordinary afternoon
near a path by an open-mouthed creek and
a playground filled with children
I watch a woman reach into her heart with gentle hands
she opens each door
the small dark door that looks like a shadow
the door locked long ago because
what was behind it terrified her
the door she bolted against fear

other poets arrive   circle her with their words
with the white spaces of their silences
where the soul of truth lives
these poets stand   go   within themselves
unlock their own doors
beckon us to see what lays behind
dark ravens of grief   iridized flight in the sun
razor rocks of pain tumble out
form the cairns stained with scarlet
point us toward our own paths

the poets rise open the doors of their darkness
become luminous within their hearts
take our hands like mothers
walk with us into our hearts
the shadow of their hands is upon our hands

In Her Studio
Linda Drajem

We intrude into a dusty silence
where light filters through
the high altar of windows over the loft.
In the chancel off to the side an acolyte
molds with his hands the brown clay
like a monk in dim candlelight.
The potter herself has left for lunch
but the pulpit is alive with her presence.
In the stark pews are unfinished pieces—
fluted columns of white
tall as a man but angled in steps,
a grey hunched phallus inviting to touch.
These are her begotten works
created out of mud and breath—
her masterpiece the squat ridges of clay lips
that laugh close to the center of a woman's body.
They ask us who have eaten the dark hours,
who trim their desires, mow down their spirit,
to come to life as the potter creates anew
in her studio holy with longing.

Word Lovers
(for Jimmie Margaret)
Linda Drajem

We count the beats
Form the sounds
Savor images large and small

Polite *c* for *can* or *could*
Sushing *s silent* and *sisterly*
Demure *t touching* and *tawny*

Toothy *ds* are diamond hard
Final as in *goodbye* and *death*
We slide our tongues on schwas
Click on capitals very properly

Capture fleet-footed moments
Scars so old they now gentle
Become like fairy-dusted pastels
Storms muffled for a brief wordy moment
Mosaics of vowels and signed endings
Drunken on their remains we celebrate

Sisters

bandaids

(for ceci)
barbara q. faust

I.

the mercurochrome-red thread opens everything
the path through childhood
the hope for healing
the snowy white square that covers the wound
the boundary between injury and air
a strip of plastic flesh to hide imperfections
carved out of a knee or elbow   by sidewalk or surgeon

II.

more than once my sister followed my mother upstairs
into the bathroom to the medicine cabinet
to watch her put the new milky bandaid tin in its place
on the glass shelf away from her little-girl reach
then my mother closed the door and left

minutes later my sister goes back alone
climbs onto the toilet into the sink to open the cupboard
　　　　to find what she needs　　to retrieve her treasure
I still see the tiny girl　a crown of golden ringlets
who arrives at the kitchen door covered
with every　*large strip　junior strip*　and *spot*
she leaves a scarlet calligraphy behind
her language strings among the bandaid papers
blanketing the white tile floor
they spell the stories she knows will come
the ones she will hide under bone　below marrow
the ones that can not be covered

Sisters Travel
Linda Drajem

In a honey-yellow kitchen of a gabled home
we watch women bake pies
of apples plucked live from the orchard
There we learn how to grow
into the aprons of our world—
hours harvesting tomatoes in the sun
vats cooking in the basement
boiling down to a blood red puree

Hand-in hand we walk from the house
away from the truck garden—
picking beans and berries
gathering eggs hot from the hen
Once lost in the woods we try to follow
boot trails of spent gunshot
left by hunters following smaller game
Leaves curled and rotting from year to year
paper over holes that become deep wells
Dark shadows loom behind old trees
and bushes rustle with ancient messages
we cannot translate

We shiver from the sound of footfalls—
barking dogs and shots firing
other paths hidden from sight
We leave trees marked with knife curls
then lose the way back till we stumble
onto a meadow a long way from home

Crossing
Kathy Shoemaker

I cross the plank over the frog pond
Clear water between me and the silty brown bottom
Leopard frogs leap freely into the elements
I find the meadow, grasses pushed every which way
Where a deer had rested. Startled to readiness
Her big eyes looked out, frightened by sudden sound,
Movement, or the acrid scent of hunters.
Was that how it was for my sister—
Prey for the boys who raped her?

Far into our future three sisters
Would hike in the mountains of Idaho
Come to a rushing creek
Two sisters laugh as they cross carelessly
Walk the virgin cedar bridge with nonchalant ease
Its roots on one side and ancient limbs on the other.

The third sister stopped, looked over to them
Her body remembering. Transmuting
To a four-legged creature of the woods
She began her journey on hands and knees—
Dropping memories into the comfort of rough-hewn bark.

The broad back of the tree steadied her to the other side
There she put her foot into the mud, left her own mark
Beside the cougar's, who must have slipped into the woods
And even now watches from behind eyes
The color of afternoon sun slanting through the forest.

Loss

Return
Linda Drajem

You'll have to take this trip with me
Remember it
You'll have to follow me
up North from sunny South
watch my bier shudder
offer me to earth
You'll have to take this trip with me
one I've taken with my mother
and now my husband
Remember it

Plant me fertile into the salty earth
near Lake Erie and the grape fields
that nourished our early years
next to the sloping farm lands—
vegetable garden all straight lines
soldier tall tomato plants
tossing maples and raspberry patch
Remember it?

You'll have to take this trip with me
watch how I weep over grave markers
drive by the old house still there
the small side door they used to wave from
my parents brown and solid as clay
now planted to bloom in that dun earth
near that rise of hill
where I will turn my shoulder
to the cold wind off the lake—
a trip you'll take one more time

poem XVIII
(for paul O)
"memory is the exercise against loss" Ruth Stone
barbara q. faust

I.
daffodil petals do shred when they die
like the last rays of the sun
that puncture the faces of dusk clouds
I've watched them this year more than any other
looking for you in this new season
sure you are near me
in some time I don't yet understand
my whole life   I was taught heaven was up
so I look for you now in air
in dawns   in sunsets when the sky is bleeding with light
I feel you sometimes near enough to touch
like that first spring night sitting on our front lawn
in the forest green Adirondack chair
your breath on my cheek
someone saying it was wind
me : silent : knowing better

II.
on my drive to work
on a spring morning in May
I am under the soft light of early time
the time of becoming   the lime powder puffs of before-leaf
          the trees pushing into sky
I wonder why mourning doves are not large
and black as crows
would they sing a fuller song
would they carry our loss on those large strong wings
          would they circle our homes
a thousand mourners   our sorrows' recognition
I wonder this on a Wednesday
when baseball is beginning to flower
the sky's clouds are a thin gruel
gauze over bright sun

you are still gone

For tomorrow
Kathy Shoemaker

I will pack the language
You once spoke
I will pack your own voice deep and resonant
Clear as the spring in the underbrush
At the foot of the hill
Up the trail through the meadow
Past flocks of bluebells—
The voice you used to speak in
Now tucked under the quilt
Your grandmother sewed for you
Blocks of tan and green
Hand-knotted with bright red yarn

Sleeping for six years now
Not as long as Rip Van Winkle
You haven't grown a long grey beard
But I do see grey appearing in your hair
It's odd to see you age as you sleep

I will pack your old personality—
The one I know so well it feels like part of me
Your laugh, your sense of humor, your glasses
All those comics you loved to read
I thought you wasted your time on
I would pack you a carton of cigarettes
And lighters, more than one
The camouflage jacket you wore
When you stood on the deck to smoke
Pressing yourself under the eaves
Away from the New England rain

I will pack the daffodils that grew
Along the back of the garage
Around the well
Down the length of the stone wall
Behind the weeping willow and the baby hemlock
You helped me move in from the woods

upon loss
(for om)
barbara q. faust

her absence is etched around your eyes now
a halo of sadness where the loss of her
has just begun to seep under your skin

this morning I hear a singer on the radio on my way to work
it is after sunrise
a line of fluorescent peach light widening at the horizon
she sings her own mother's absence
I think of you the freshness of your sorrow
as the clouds lift the shade of day

there are so few places where we can just breathe
where we can relax into oursleves
the woman talks between her songs
of wanting her mother back for just one moment
of wanting her mother to hold her for just one more moment
tonight I watch your face
the distance of your smile
your gaze into the air that is her empty space
I wish you breath

If she didn't have a calendar
Kathy Shoemaker

Would she know you had died
One hundred eleven days ago?

Would it matter that it's coming up on six months
As a friend told her this morning
Meaning to comfort with information
That six months is a mark
An anniversary, a place
In the process of grieving
Where all can find her.

If they read self-help books on grief
Everyone will know exactly where she is on her path
Will know she has made the forced march onward
Left her own trail of bright red berries
Blood that fed him
When he was inside of her.

Goodbye Dream
Linda Drajem

Death takes her time for you
so skilled in winning battles
years working into each night
days crammed to the brim
with skirmish after skirmish
Now your war diminished to dining
on meals of egg custards
cups of cool vanilla cream
spooned into your shriveled lips
that close like a purse after each thrust

You hold tight to the smiles of a nurse
a white haired son who tends you
a grandson's hand whose name you forgot
a multicolored quilt from a faraway friend
Every Sunday the priest brings a wafer
reminds you of something you once knew
vaulted cathedrals and incense
a distant whisper of memory
Neither the shouts of the woman next door
nor the oppressive bodies so close
disturb this serious business
Eyes need to open each morning
watch the sun dribble through cheap cotton
taste a measure of morphine under the tongue

You prepare for a passage that lurks
body curling to shape of the past
the cocoon that cradles the sores
Your thinning arms circle each moment
wave goodbye with a small smile
then the firm closing of lips
to all gifts of food while the pulse
flutters like an uncertain bird
at the shadowed guest's greeting
What do you see beyond us
in the dream you know is waiting
after busy years with no time to reflect
—no time to just be

LOVE

j, still and always
barbara q. faust

I slip your socks on late in the night
like a winter fog   they wrap each pale toe   each sole
within the warmth you left for me below our quilt
when you returned to your own country
Neruda wrote once about woolen fish   sapphire blue
but I fly in your socks
through deep and deeper gray trusting the way
soul radar   the path to your arms a hundred miles from here
each night I journey
through cloud   through breath to you
this has always been the way we move
parallel ribbons of electric sunrise
that tie and unloose
like a beating and resting heart
creating the soft nest   the rosebud of an infant grin
the loon's song
the fragile turquoise of hours

The Dancing
Linda Drajem

We dance the cha-cha in the dim lights
of my parents' house one day in 1964.
The record blares *oh baby oh baby*
do you wanna dance and we cling tight
floating around their living room
on the rose rug already threadbare
from so many steps so many broken rules.
After an embrace it's time to go
and we begin to plan tomorrows
in the hall next to the shuttered milk-box
under a square of light from a naked bulb.

Then a future twirls in our heads
before sick babies and a dying father
before one son in Africa,
and one across the continent.
Aches of age grow in rooms we build
and some friends pass too soon.
Now the morning sky looks bruised;
a moonlight rim slips through the window.
In our own house we fold into each other
each night to dream the cha-cha
as we wait for those next steps;
Do you wanna dance oh baby

Small Bits of Happiness
Kathy Shoemaker

This morning we looked ahead
Into the harbor over mugs of coffee
Nothing to see except water
Until we spotted a small boat
Towing a loaded barge toward the horizon—
Through the break-wall a sailboat.

In the evening a simple dinner
Hummus and pita
Fresh tomatoes
Raw carrots
Wine
The earth in our supper.

Tonight we talk of old age
Of floating off spaceship earth
Sense the tether grow more tenuous
More fragile.

Look back over our shoulders
Remember the morning
Cormorants gathering breakfast
Gulls circling rising floating up
Like white confetti.

Linda Drajem,

For Mark and Christopher
and their families

For Bob—let the dancing continue.

Yesterday

Fire Dream

"The dark vital root within us all ..."
  Carlo Levi

In the beginning was the tree
tossing in the window on the hill
next to the farm house—
with its awful roots down deep
and the little girl watching the tossing tree
with its roots down deep
next to the house on the lonely hill.

The little girl afraid watching the tree
that night in the old house on the hill
and on the hill the barn alive with horses.
Firelight and shouts, horses stomping
before the fire that would consume
the house on the hill, on that lonely hill.
The fire will roar and eat up
the barn and the tree with its roots—
awful roots throbbing down deep
holding on to the toes of the world
down deep where the fire
flamed and pushed out the house.

The house will dance in the flames
and the tree will have arms of fire.
The little girl watches the tree
and dreams of the fire to come.

The fiery hands, the screaming horses
and she goes into a deep trance
going into her own roots
which throb and ache; her eyes
will be awake—alive—awake
but she will see nothing, nothing
except the horses stomping
and the cows mutely loving the flames
loving the searing fire; taking it in
lowing in murmuring moans.

The girl will sing in her trance
speak tongues, cry, shout
and will not awake from the dream;
the dream burning in her
throbbing roots; the roots down deep.

Tea Parties with Gram

They were for looking only
those delicate china cups
red-gold filigree from pre-war Japan
along with the ruby wine glasses
the coins from Austria
Papa got in the Alps during the war
On the wall sepia drawings
of places she would never see—
the Coliseum, the Forum, Mt Etna
though looking was her specialty

We had tea served in dime store cups
with cracked bowls and missing handles
sweet cake twisters from Wedell's bakery—
her world shrunk to these celebrations
by useless legs no longer good for action
Crocheted flowers and fluted leaves
emerged from hands gnarled like the bulbs
of gladiolus languishing in the garden
her husband planted and ignored
This patch of new hope
she still allowed herself in a life trimmed
to small dimensions

Just as Night Fell

Just as night fell we'd play
hide and seek under the street lamp
each night in ritual recite the rules
sure we never would remember it all
two brothers from across the street
                    my sister and I
(proud to be included with the boys)
and Joe of the stuttering walk
would mow over us
with his barrage of words
that being his game
since a bad leg prevented heavier sports

We'd hide in Mr. Smith's bushes
                    across the street
or in the vacant lot back of Mike the Greek's
who made cherry cokes
                    on Tonawanda St
or behind the show secretly watching
                    violent sunsets

It was a quiet time   a holding time
Families would gather on the porch
to watch us   drinking their beer
telling jokes and analyzing the news
Every Sunday we'd pray after Mass
that great demon Russia would release
                    the captive nations
and we didn't see how tied we were
to the rules written large inside us

We children would weave in and out
of dying light
          trying to get home-free
to be the first one to name it
and only decades later are we close

Old Photo

I see you standing there in the garden
with a rosebud smile eager to please
blinking into new spring light
on your confirmation day.
The old ritual beckons—
the blow on the cheek from the bishop
prayer books with praise for the Father
gifts of rosary chains.

Nearby is the rosebush
freed from the jar where it spent the winter
thorny arms and lush leaves slashed
captured under the canning glass
till loosened to grow spindly each spring.

Soon you will leave that yard,
rituals will pale, rosary beads fray
jars may even split—
let the rose bloom thick and wild.
No more need for trimmed arms
protection from the snow—
no more shadows asking to be safe.

Sicilian Visit: Serradifalco

The home of the falcons
flying over the rolling hills
that slope over to the Ionian Sea
rows of graped fences
a tumble of earthen buildings
five dogs on the street baking in sun

In the grey steel commune among dun stones
ancient ledgers speak of poverty—
contadina and *casalingua* who fled
fly specked doorways draped in canvas
lost fathers and weeping mothers
among the olive groves
grape fields belonging to the landlord

A place to leave the past
create a new story to tell
far from goat milk and sharp cheese
peaches and blood oranges
the native born *nespali*
a fruit both sour and sweet

Fairy Tale

Aunt Rosetta gave Grandma
satin shoes for her wedding day
It was April, buds pushed out
and crocuses breached the cold earth
Grandma rode the carriage to church
white lace banded about her head
and tight on her tiny wrists
She began to weep when fat snowflakes
out of season dripped like her tears
After the shoes were stained
with cracked heart shapes—
but she kept them in her closet
danced in them every night
during frenzied dreams
Each morning her legs ached
she had a dry and hopeless cough
Her daughter took the shoes
wore them for a walk into dark woods
where strange men said keep dancing

The Opening

for me it was E.E. Cummings
to let in the light
on a tightly packaged girlhood

sister Bea looked on in disdain
plucked away the poetry book
nestled between leaves of geometry

shook the silver cross
on her robed bosom
restrained and taped down like the rules
inhaled along with chalk dust

how
        worthless
                such foolery

those *anyones who lived in pretty how towns*
to fracture perfect symmetry of faith
but E.E. had done his damage

One Gift

Each night outside my window you watch
while brazenly I shed my clothes
sure I would never be anxious like Mother
or cautious like Father in the larger world.
With open arms I toss blouse, underwear, stockings
to flutter free like leaves on the dying elms.
New breasts greet the air without flinching
that cold November before I left that cozy world.

When your tracks appear at my window
I who had never known fear shudder
pretend to read while a neighbor hides
to chase the intruder.
Hands shake as I try to dial for help,
words come out in garbled chunks
mined carelessly from an old quarry.
Then you become prey too.

You go free but give me the gift
that trimmed and shaped a growing girl—
a legacy that links us all these years.

Pulse of Light

A square of butter on the wall
each morning as I wake
Last night it bloomed electric
in a corner till past midnight
Today it embraces trees
showers the wind swept leaves
with squares of blessing
strains through stretched clouds
twisted firm like the sheets my mother
washed over the battered tin tubs
in the dark basement of the old house
She lifted them in panes of sparkling water
before the violent shift to the wringer—
where one time I caught my finger
and cried *Mama* to her delight—
before she carried them in wicker baskets
to hang and flutter in early fall heat
capturing a sheaf of sunbeams—
a bright gladdened moment
for those dancing white flags
tethered to earth by knots and poles
dividing the day with hanging up
and taking down in predictable rhythm
A ritual of inhaling scents
and the sun's buttery claims

Voices

Penelope's Sisters

We weave and unweave—
We sweep floors stained again
by boots fresh from battle
nurse babies who cry for others
tend the old whose needs expand
A cycle of doing and undoing
like Penelope at her labors
unraveling the pieces of herself
in the upstairs room

Penelope builds no temples
no skyscrapers or bombs
takes no unfettered journeys
She weaves fanciful threads
into tapestry that rise from dreams—
hangings of multicolored webs
only to pull out the garlands
that twist and turn and fall
useless by the door each morning
We know her song in our bones
the marrow of our flattened desires

Our story hides in the return—
the drama of battles and gods' disguises
for the old inflated honor and glory
but homely works, done and undone
merit barely a line in the tale
Penelope must sweat and push again—
create the fabric of everyday colors
until all that remains is the shawl
drawn about worn shoulders

One Hundred Killed Near the Mexico Border

We are the nameless
We are the women of the border
We are the tossed away
Who left our homes never to return
Young and pretty but dark of skin and poor
Our families ask for answers
But police laugh and politicians ignore
We are the questions
That prick the conscience then drain away

We leave for school never to return
Or board rickety buses for the *maquiladoras*
We work with our hands
Place widgets in wiper blades at Trico
Sew dresses for the women in the cities
Solder doors of Ford trucks
Dance topless in the clubs of Juarez
To serve the stateside boys

We are the old before our time
Going back to rusted trailers without water
Or shacks in garbage dumps
We are rotting in mesquite desert
Or worse returned a mutilated corpse
Without the dignity of a fine dress
Or a pine box to be resurrected without glory
To fathers too poor to ask why
To mothers too beaten to say
No ,she is not who you say
In life she is a *Vivianna,* or *Alma,* or *Elizabetta*
A beloved daughter who deserves a name

Massuod's Wife

(Ahmed Shah Massuod was assassinated near the Tajik
border on Sept 9, 2001)

Behind her burkha she grieves
For the husband blown up by the betrayers
His eyes running out of his head
Every inch of skin ruptured
Two pieces of metal lodged in his heart
She grieves that the thirty seconds left alive
He did not call for her but for Fahim
The son who fought by his side
She grieves for her lonely nights before
When he recited Persian poetry with friends
She grieves for the warrior of faith
Who fasted and prayed five times a day
Who never let the sun fall on her uncovered head

The Lion of Panshir Valley who spent his life
Committed to jihad will never come to her rooms
Will never touch her again to produce more sons
Who ring the table like olive trees in desert winds
No one asks for the wife of Massuod
She grieves silent in her burkha
Walking the rooms of the family compound
Invisible in the purdah of a woman's life
Who knows of her words
Who celebrates her life
Who carries her image in parades in Kandahar
Her life hidden behind a blue burkha

Auguste Deter

told the doctor at the clinic
I have lost myself
That was one hundred years ago

Dr Alzheimer would go on to watch her die
in a fog of empty words and incoherent screams
a bedridden husk with layers of her former self
shed on the floor of a stinking room
The good doctor looked inside her brain
for answers to this strange disease
He sliced and diced frozen slivers
and through the new fangled microscope
emerged a mass of tangled threads
In magical magenta stain
weedy mean strands showed brilliant
nestled between neurons so comfortable
so choking that Auguste disappeared

The good doctor lives on to frighten us
who lose the keys or drop a word
inside the stained cells of aging brains

In the Strawberry Fields of Gaza

My four sons play marbles
Fields of plush hearted berries
Wave and ask to be harvested
Every day they play while we weed
Fertilize with sweat the winding tresses
Of fragile plants pushing toward sun
It was a day like every other

Or no other
Suddenly the mortar shell whirls
Lands with sharp gasp and then thunder
The earth shakes and my sons flew up
Land like butchered lambs in spring
On the greenhouse the head of Farad
Abdullah's hands wave in a tree
Here is your third son said a farmer
As I gather my bitter harvest
A young girl calls to me
Why are you collecting meat my mother

Ahmad asks for his brothers from his bed
Head fevered and wounds dressed
In the fields, I say, *in the strawberry fields*
With the fruit red as blood

The Women's Underworld

In the nursing home
the women travel to dine
in wheelchair chariots that gleam
They wear pastel stretch pants
cotton sweaters and velcro sneakers
In the dining room
the servers prepare places—
tie blue terrycloth bibs
around nodding white heads
that bob like trees too tired for storms
Aides serve cocktails of watered juice
and soup without a name

In the nursing home
they light candles every night
to shine on parchment skin
like suns that waver in the fetid air
Each morning waiting souls line the halls—
some shout above the click of wheels
some see beyond barren walls
back to days when they posed in high heels
pencil thin hose and silk dresses

Machines buzz and whir—
carts screech as the women ferry rivers
cram the halls nodding in their chairs
Aides present offerings in paper cups
pomegranate seeds for ancient mothers—
one bows to the gods she missed
one cries *come here come here*
one chants her mystic song
in somber twilight sliding into sleep

Sabah's Story

They beat him for marrying me,
they berate me for loving him,
—lines of hatred carved across our hearts.
In widow's black I watch from behind corners,
think of that day they finally free us.
He walks away on legs damaged from torture
only to sink to his knees facing Mecca
while shots ring out again.

They captured us and put us into a trunk
in front of the crowd on the Bagdad street.
Shia and Sunni we lived and loved for years
but the world walks in with force
shuffles us from abandoned school
to policeman's home, to bare basement
—not strangers but my people.

Now in the armoire hangs his wedding suit,
on the bureau the cigarette lighter,
a brush and comb just as he left them
that fateful day we ventured out
like newlyweds eager for a summer's lark
in a city we called home.

Woman Wings

what wings I have
sprout through edge of skin
slice the close air
swirl in a grenadine sunset
to reach some far horizon
these wings have taken long to unfurl
these wings have folded up
under buffeting winds
writhed in phantom pain
these wings have been beaten back
clipped and razored
to an edge of their buds
waited waited
but would not stop
the long slow leaning into light
would not refuse to grow again
—poor battered sprites
after battles, slights, blows
—poor blighted nubs
lean into moonrise
dance alive in dawn's blushing glow

Today

Heart Pictures

In a converted garage off the doctor's office
the technician with rolled yellow hair
and red painted nails on chubby hands
rubs a gel onto my stippled cold chest.

I watch the picture unfold its mysteries,
marvel at the little valve smiling into the camera
like a happy rabbit wriggling its muscled foot
silent as it works—
it does not stop and I am glad.

The technician calls me *honey* and *sweetie*
though I am old enough to be her mother—
she complains of the cold
she complains of the snow
she complains of the work.
My valve ignores her and beats away
thrumming fast in a dizzy dance.

Then she moves the magic wand to my neck
and a roar rises in an eager cacophony
streaming up the artery to meet the brain,
pushed by that rabbit foot heart
singing its hymn of survival.
Now I love her but she does not know,
folds her angel wings for another patient
who shivers outside the door waiting to see.

Winter Morning

"I didn't even guess I was happy."
    Linda Pastan

After the solstice the house empty at last
breathes out and in   while I search
for the gold coin misplaced so long ago.
There was a joy in wiping noses, telling stories,
rubbing firm the counter tops, lacing white the windows.
The scents of fresh linen mingle with chicken soup
                    on a back burner.
Did I know I was happy? Fragile faces of those I love
move on to manage alone and I tidy words
as my mother did drawers   or   cupboards empty,
singing   under my breath   lost in the flow.
The plant I tried to kill now branches out green
by my feet   enjoying a blast of winter air.
My books curl around me   papers slide away
and I wonder if this will be a moment
that I remember   some place far away.
when crows bellow loud ,calling us all
to know here and now: we are.

Ours—Celebrating Adoption Day

You are ours before you came to us
You chose your family and we waited
with aching empty arms
Then your dads looked into your eyes
and knew—you are ours
That first November day we visited
rocked you on Great-Grandma's chair
wrapped you in blankets lent by others
We said—you are ours

That first Christmas aunts and cousins
welcomed you into the folds of winter love
When spring came we took residence
warm in your family's embrace
lucky to share daily smiles and coos
walks on the beach, trips to the zoo
listening to the penguins' sad song
the elephants' call and response

At your first birthday hats and balloons
laughter, candles and cries
By Thanksgiving a favorite song is *Cows*
and *musik* the refrain every car trip time
Pops holds you longer than he has to
you pat his neck and snuggle closer
Grammy hears you tap the bedroom door
soon croon together in pale new light
Then that second birthday
we sing you into a third year
You are ours
And now— we are yours

Florida Visit With Babies

Miss Zoe McZoe does her dance near supper
Mr No No joins with twirls and laughs
embracing after a nap time apart

We the audience for the performance
often join in improvising steps
to follow their tiny feet
sing out of tune to all but their ears

After macaroni and cheese
after applesauce with orange slices
we carry the pails and shovels to the beach
There we dig and pat and build—
castles and birthday cakes
find shells of furled pink whorls
count pelicans and sanderlings
play choo-choo grabbing tails of shirt
—a line of fools in blazing light
until our shadows lengthen
until the sun crashes into the sea

We drag the pails and shovels back
to dance some more
then to dream the dance again

Country of Strangeness

We've entered the archway.
We've long passed a portal.
The willow tree trails yellow leaves
for the last time.
Apples are rotted and gnawed
at the base of the gnarled trunk.
The finch sings off key, the cardinal silent,
tomatoes stay green and wither on the vine.
What harvest there is has been gathered.

My father totters out to greet me
hair askew, bits of beard escaping,
grooming last on his list now.
Mother gives something each visit,
yellowed tablecloth from the her wedding,
cracked leather gloves stored in mothballs,
golden bracelet for a first great grandchild.

When did it change?
When did they stop being who I remember—
twin sequoias, bulwarks of strength,
first to share who they were.

Each day my mother finds celebration—
the photo of a great grandchild,
the cleaning lady's visit,
Sister Clara bringing communion.
Each day my father says he sits
to study maple leaves turning.
When did the long goodbyes
turn into the air we breathe.

March Light

I
Drips like mercy unfolding,
a gift we scarcely believe is real
when sun glints off melting ice
in a fragile eggshell sky.
Today the man in an apron
crumbles bread for the pigeons.
They wait for me,
then the storm of their delight.
In a parking lot, light makes me dizzy,
I back into a car with sickening screech.
A young woman opens her door,
but she smiles and we embrace.

II
Black helicopters churn the air,
share the sky with a flock of geese.
Fog pools around tall buildings,
muffled up and silent as robed cars
slide down shrouded streets.
Figures dart in between the panels of white
while wind whips the barren trees.
Clouds are swept away in rampages,
marching like an army across military sky.
Ice flows push through blankets of cold
revealing patches of clear waves.

III
Across the yard yellowed grass tries to green,
square jawed pine pushes out fingers of growth.
Daffodils and narcissus pokes fresh shoots,
sun drains through a scrim of clouds
and seeps into winter worn windows.
Light becomes a long taper of hope.

Monuments

They lie in the bottom of a drawer
flutter out on butterfly wings
a sift of papers from his life—
receipt for the home he tended
last will leaving meager gifts
eulogy from his church service
Now he is a decay of bones
in the cemetery I pass each week
on the way to see my mother
I almost forget how he wandered
lost in the memory of our old home
when we were young and juicy with love

I pull out the desk drawer
made perfectly balanced
caressed with wood stain
and polished caramel gold
carved out of his sweat
That last gift given
before his lungs scarred
his arm useless by his side
his memory seared away
no longer able to turn the key
Now other parchment leaves lie
at ease on the bottom desk drawer

October

elbows her way into our lives
too soon too soon we say
Days and weeks turn into themselves
—too soon too soon
First she arrives in a clutch of clouds
rumpling white in a sky backlit golden
later on grey with the bang of thunder
lightening spikes and a rush of rain

The veins of the city pulse
across a field of cornflowers
Monarch butterflies wave their arms
in the journey homeward
—*don't leave so soon* we say
practice swirling like the geese
But we know they will not stay
just as time will not slow
or dried heads of hydrangea
survive the coming winter
We hope the butterflies
so hungry for the pinched face of sun
will evade dark dressed famine
with her witch's hat
even when October becomes
a dead heap of days

For a Moment

There on the Bayou Teche
all seems possible
Egrets like prehistoric clouds
ease over the brown water
lazy in the Louisiana sun
while the aged Romero Brothers
strum on guitars in twin harmony
wailing Cajun love songs

One offers me his chair
and I an audience of one clap
as swallows swoop over water
alive and etched in ink
On the Bayou Teche the wind slows
to caress the dying azalea blooms
Another song gloats over the soft rise
of live oaks and dripping moss
while the sun loves the water
and the embracing air is soft

Later we tour the shrines of our youth
remember there our children played
remember they first rode a bike
remember we flew kites in that meadow
We spend the night at Mrs. Martin's inn
near high standing graves on watery earth
protecting her decayed ancestors

All night the trucks rumble loud on the way
to Lafayette to Baton Rouge to New York
In the morning she leaves a silver tray
by our oak carved door
coffee rich as midnight
bread so light it flutters in our hands
There on the Bayou Teche
far away from all need
the morning sun washes away the dew
even the graveyard looks fresh
beside the slumbering waters

We Think the World Alive

for Robert

My husband has the numbers—
equations for triangles, cylinders, squares
dance in his brain.
I call to him before the telephone,
What's the number?
now lost in my brain's lobes and folds
Instead I consume words
sometimes in an eager rush,
other times a struggle to string
across the page freed from snares
making their way home.
I think them in chunks and towers
that spill from books
or push into the square slots of puzzles.

In the airport, in the market place,
he counts in sixes and sevens
to whisper in our grandbaby's ear.
Balloons become colliding circles,
buildings broken into intersecting planes.
On the map he imposes geometric
precision for rolling roadways.
With the toddler he counts her steps
giving his gifts to the future.
Sometimes they float under dreams,
make him sit up and say yes
to his story a feast of numbers
while my words tell a different tale.

barbara q. faust

these poems are for
the women whose shadows I walk in
the women I dance with now and
the women-to-be I hear
skipping behind me
and for j

what is real
(for j)

I think it was on a Tuesday morning
although it could have been a Wednesday afternoon
it was summer
the tomatoes were scarlet   full of themselves
ready to explode
the basil was emerald green
the mint was soft as my daughter's skin
when she took my hand in her two-year-old fingers
so long ago
the morning glories swirled closed
like blueberry custard twirled with vanilla
because they are never selfish about staying past their time
the air smelled of cut grass
the way it did at that first cutting way back in springtime
we walked past the frittilaria
early flowers that stand low to the ground
reticulated petals of mauve and cream
like barely opened umbrellas
I think we sat together side by side
on the front porch in the deep green Adirondack chairs
we looked to each other at the same time and smiled
I think our fingertips touched

I remember
it was just that simple

shake hands

we are taught early how to shake hands
how to clasp others'   keep our grasp firm
show we are present but just for the moment

just once   what if we held each other longer
what if we held each other
long enough to begin to dissolve into each other
rest our skin upon each other's
become one skin   so the blood cleansed by my heart
fills your fingertips as they hold me

when I was small
I stood for lifetimes on the sand at the edge of the sea
palms of ocean came again and again
lay themselves on my toes on the tops of my feet
urging me into the embrace of the sea
a thousand times I remained long enough
to give myself to salt of that sea to become land and water

so today take my hand   hold it
wait   stay   wrap your fingers around mine
I will wrap mine around yours   feel our palms touch
we melt into the rises and valleys of each other's skin
our lifelines and the whorls of our fingertips spiral together
the touch of my fingers is yours
within the small curve of this embrace   the arc of this wave
the ebb and flow of our tide
we are one journey

about time

I am terrified   we have forgotten
how to measure our days in clouds
forgotten to use the wash of cirrus
the whipped domes of cumulus   to mark the hours
we no longer remember to count minutes
in the petals of spring tulips
in the toad lilies that hide their speckled orchid faces
      in the garden's early autumn shade
we do not see there are calendars
in the altars of each rock
carved by the turquoise of glacial lakes
we do not hear time call us
from the ancient bodies of glaciers
who roar and show us their summer-sky blue flesh
as they calve

today   we count our days in numbers in guns and bombs
      in the contents of our banks
we do not remember how long time is
      when we watch handfuls of clouds
      scatter like cotton balls
      travel summer's azure sky in a kaleidoscope of white
yet   we have only to fog a mirror with our breath
to find that time in its clearing

international women's day, 1994
"Getting old is just a matter of getting easier to see through."
Barbara Kingsolver

maps of blue veins
tracts of time run   north   south
on the arms of wisdom
her life spelled in sapphire calligraphy
on wrinkled parchment skin

each year her veins rise   like bread
ripen to braille so the blind can read her journey
her peach flesh hangs away from the ivory bones
where it is draped like velvet curtains
rods exposed
she walks through her days
a topographical lifescape
for those who follow behind her

to THE women

you teach me
the way to hold my ordinary days up like a monstrance
        golden in Easter Sunday light
to laugh and dance my way into the waxing of each full moon
you hold my life's secrets and pain in your hands
understanding both are glass globes
blown large and fragile with the breath of my passions
spun wild with the force of my demons
you see beauty in the contours of rage
when I shatter   the scarlet   the milk glass   the ruby
when poison spills out and I am dying   within my life
you take me by the hand
tell me to look at the blood flowing from my wounds
like red silk you say *warm red silk*
then you paint my face   the amethyst of the first crocus
the butter yellow of daffodils
the incarnadine from the first poppies of June
you trace the Pleiades on my left cheek
        so I carry my starsisters through daylight
you draw a rose on each fingertip of my writing hand
        so I remember to write petals and thorns
you dress me in garments of light
so I will not forget sun
so I will remember to dance

I adorn myself
(for cheryl jordan)

within a winter morning
the snowy light of moonset spills inside two homes
puddles in two small rooms
onto the ebony and milk of two faces

we adorn our arms and the shells of our ears
with rings of silver   bone   bronze
with cowrie shells
with the mottled incarnadine stones of a woman's life
with gems the color of a late summer day
blessings from mothers and grandmothers
our ancestor-women who prepare to arrive again
on the winter solstice
with ruby velvet bags that hold their hearts
embroidered with the stories we tell again and again
of scarlet lipstick rings on a glass of beer
of the first music of silver bracelets

their stories become our poems
weave themselves into the garments
we wrap around ourselves   to keep our selves
they are our music   we are their dancers
we whirl to the breath of our mothers
pirouette to the songs of our grandmothers   our sisters
we swirl scarves of blood red
and earth green that tell everything
in clouds of words   that are our amulets

these women bless our days we sing their ancient songs
we sing our new songs of our silences
of the silences of our sisters
whose worlds are the color of terror
whose mirrors have no faces
when the dance is over
I see your soul in my mirror   it is the halo around my face

the gift of silence
(for j)

you watch me
during quiet beach walks
wordless Sunday morning *reads* on the front porch
hikes filled with the leathery rhythm of footsteps
wakings to the music of a gaze
              arms wrapped around each other

you take this silence
the kind stars live in   the kind poppies unfurl in
wrap it in a simple blue box
the color of the sky above the sea
place it in my hands
knowing I understand

you take me into stillness where I see
the loons' mating dance
watch water create crystal beads along wildflower stems
              that stand in a glass vase of cobalt blue
learn the petroglyphs left by
              Native people hundreds of years ago
know the calving of a glacier
understand a tiny garden of herbs
              luminous in rain below a dark sky
taste a matte green bowl filled with
              the glistening flesh of peaches
              listen to them sing *summer summer*
              through their furred mouths
read the stories of sandpipers scribed upon a beach

I speak another language

herb gathering
"I will remember the last light on the lowest branch"
Muriel Rukeyser

as I will remember a Sunday morning in midsummer when
we went out before breakfast to pick herbs from our garden
I will remember the dark sky   the sheets of rain
the herbs glowing chartreuse
as though it is early spring again
I will see your bare toes and
the glow of my scarlet-tipped ones
safe in your ebony strapped sandals
against my summer brown skin
lest I slip and fall along our path
you will stand on the threshold
unfurling the black umbrella   outside to preserve our luck
you will step into the rain   wait for me to join you
I will see the steps we take together to rain music
I will bend to our small patch of herbs   ruffled parsley
the long hair of the chives
the emerald basil
whose lacy leaves were already someone's meal
the fragrant needles of rosemary
the few amethyst leaves of opal basil
the soft licorice stems of tarragon
damp and glistening with rain
I will remember pinching off ruffles of parsley first
as you ask *which part of you would you like me to cover*
while you adjust the umbrella over us
I will remember not choosing rosemary that morning
because it was too far into the garden to reach
I will see myself stepping onto the porch
to pinch the soft jade needles of tarragon
while you wait unbrellaed and barefoot in the grass
later I will remember warm mouthfuls of summer herbs
folded into the soft sun of Sunday morning eggs

appletime
(for lucille clifton)

doesn't it take such a *damn* long time to ripen
doesn't it make you jealous
of the breasts of sungold mangos
and the sharp sweetness of autumn apples
who come into themselves in just one summer
don't you remember   that time   that green time
that bright-green-of-first-spring   time
how you knew summer would follow soon
how you would walk   ripe and juicy through this world

I am beginning to feel my green places deepen to crimson
below fingernail moons on late summer nights
I am beginning to feel my flesh yield
to the gentle pressure of someone's fingers
like papaya and starfruit
I am   becoming
the tart crisp mouthful
who will not dissolve into you quietly
will not slip away easily
without a few loud crunches

the basket

I want to weave my own basket
from the amethyst of the first iris
the sapphire of the night sky
the ruby threads of the bloodsilk I once made
below the pearl face of the moon
I want to fill long scarlet afternoons
weave thread round and round through the ivory of my fingers

I will fill the basket with warm eggs from a rainbow of hens
celadon   café au lait   milky rose orbs
that continue time   comfort everyone who still worries
about whether the ruffled hen or the tiny ovoid came first

in this real time I am alone
within the whiteness of an early spring morning
in the time of afterdawn when no birds sing
when the only sounds are the flying clouds of my exhalations
the scrape of my shovel   digging   digging
searching for the beginning of poppies
the furred emerald fingers of promise

in this milky silence I need to ribbon sound to the last memory
tie it to the incarnadine patches of poppy skins
scattered across an earthen bed
wounds from a dying summer   a thousand lifetimes ago

fingertip learning

a poet once said
when you grow old enough
you learn your life through your fingertips
you learn summer   picking the satin leaves of basil
          grasping the soft surprise of tarragon needles
you learn late July as red and purple raspberries
          bleed on your fingers   stain the whorls
          and spirals of your touch
you learn sadness in the limp embrace of a four year old
          whose brown arms just lay on your shoulders
          whose tears come through your blouse
          sink into your skin
you learn love in the patty cake of two infant hands
          that find they have a partner
in the first-day-of-school hug of a five-year-old
          you have known since she was three
in the surprise of heat
when a hand touches muscle tendon skin
          along the back of your neck
          as you drive through the the crunch of sapphire air
          into the mountains
          below the ruby and gold of the autumn maples

woman's work

they would have us believe
our work is ironing pillowcases upside down
the paternal name rises
engraves our cheeks in the night
we are branded in our dreams

we know our heat—
it is inside our words—it is our stories
they arrive in scarlet and saffron
spin themselves into tapestry with turquoise and jade
this is our work—we name the colors of truth

the crimson of a single mother's eyes
who carries her flailing son home
because he cannot finish another day at school

the grape flower on a wife's cheek
after she has bumped into another door

the ebony characters of a religious book
crawling along the skin of a woman
someone else's truth defining her as property

in this world scribes are murdered   carved up
like the supper she cannot make
one more night

dreaming

open your hand
lay the shimmer in your palm
close your fingers around it   it is your heart

the open face of the moon
travels like night milk into your window
lays herself down—makes a pool on your bed

come into darktime
she is your place to swim until waking
your place to nourish dreams
wrap your mind in velvet
dance the truths of your life
pirouettes of ruby mangos
the pax de deux of pale beach roses
splash your dreaming self with their petals
see the beauty of your bones through skin
solid moonlight   the strong calligraphy of your skeleton
the scaffold for your hours
the frame for each breath

in white space

"You still think of those who
have died, and I tell you, *'Don't worry,*
we still have their absence,'"
                    Susan Griffin

long before you died and I learned to hold your absence
I worked at the art gallery
I learned whitespace from sculptures

I see the oval and triangular places
alive in a small bronze dancer by Degas
who wears a real pink tutu and satin ballet slippers
I know a sculpture by the front door
a large black rose bush in winter
on the tour for the visually impaired
I travel within its spaces through its branches
around its thorns
I feel the parallelograms   the trapezoids of air
the way I touch the long ellipse of breath Degas created
within the arms of his dancer clasped behind her back
the tall triangle of her bronze legs

I never write   within the whitespaces   of someone's poems

the consequences of a change in routine

late in the milk of winter mornings or
in the center of sun-drenched summer afternoons
I lay my pen down   close my journal
begin to put my words away
I take the ones I love first
cerulean   incarnadine or
the ones that explain the iron lace in the marrow of a woman
I put them in the silken bag
of turquoise saffron and coral
pack them away until I need to tell another story

but this last time I forgot
I left words scattered in a hundred places
they are lost   and I am looking for them everywhere
I hope I put *scarlet* and *breath* in that place
next to the perfect Christmas gift
I bought for my daughter in March but forgot in December
I think I left the metaphors in the attic
near the waffle iron or   if not I'm certain they must be
in the school box with the fingerpaints
and the long pipe cleaners
but where are *emerald* and *milky* and *sargasso*
I need *sargasso* to describe this thick-aired afternoon
where there are no poems
only this dark air I cannot force into my lungs
this late day darkness I cannot see through
to find *poppy* or *wind* or
the phrase *tiny doughy fingers*
I keep searching   searching   lost as my words

finding the language

the words gather themselves   my trade beads
   invisible   distant   unimportant
I string them together   try to make beauty out of truth
but without the thread of my own language
I cannot link them   cannot bracelet   my wrist
my neck   my fingers

the words fall from my palm
roll down across the oak floors
under the old pine apothecary which will not be moved
they roll into the fireplace
incinerated before they are found
they shatter upon impact
I am empty-handed without the knotted language
that gives me directions
shows me the way to myself again
shows me the phrases that fasten together   that say
turn left   walk forward
notice the sunrise
watch snowy cloud puffs backlit by the cobalt of a dusk sky
remember to go into the garden
collect the dried seeds of the cosmos
rub them between your palms
scatter them into the empty corners of your garden
be their wind

I am directionless
I cannot see myself in the mirror when I open my eyes
I forget how to use the language I have built
how to climb the bone scaffold
how to stand tall within this mid-summer sky

the archeologist

once I thought I could be an archeologist
discover what lay forgotten below years under breathing
inside months
> *a maroon tricycle frozen in amber*
>> *beside a pair of red Keds®*
> *the fragments of a white Wedgwood bowl wreathed in gray*
>> *sent by a cousin from England*
> *Thanksgiving dinners with the hot fudge sauce made*
>> *in my grandmother's ancient double boiler*

this is my civilization my soul's village
the place I travel to dig up my history of home
of towns   of roads   of stories

this Monday night in autumn
when the leaves of the sugar maple hang like bloody palms
I excavate word after word
I come to the tip of *this* memory   long buried   jagged
dangerous in the soft soil of the poem
my words are the sable bristles cleaning off the last layers
removing time from this relic
I lift it into my hands   I am still wounded by its edges
I bring it to my face for one last inhalation
lay it back where I cannot reach it
cover it with words   deep within a long poem

thanksgiving
"the bowl was smooth, silver-gray and quite deep"
Ann Goldsmith

once you brought me
a black and white photograph of an eggshell
it was inside a book   telling how chickens are born
the photograph was magnified

it is the pits and roughness of this November sky
that blankets this spring morning before Thanksgiving
when we run outside between raindrops
to remember we will not melt
to taste the last glimpses of rosy petunias
and the suns of marigolds
who have already lived through frost

this time   before crystal pellets of rain
sends us inside again
we ring arosy around the puddles
we race to the maple tree
where the last golden rags of leaves
hang from chicken-footed branches
we catch drops on our tongues

I am thankful you continue to teach me
to taste each day as though my tongue is a rose petal

the truth about zero
(for sally)

a poet once said she loved
what she couldn't see in a photograph
the truth you trust in order to understand beauty
the one you weave into your heart
where its beating is the night music that keeps your fear away
the empty spaces hold everything important
the corner of you where zero isn't nothing
it is the empty set

truth is the chartreuse taste of
       spring grass on your four year old tongue
is the milky towel that smells of autumn sun on your hands
       as you fold loopy exclamations of cotton
       into thirds the way your mother did
is the jagged calligraphy on
       a summer sidewalk whose poems can terrify
       the rusted touch of farewell blood
       warm silk along your thighs
       truth incarnadine

the world spins as slowly as breathing
           fills your lungs
           keeps you singing

for the bone doctor

it was not the first slim tibia
lying beside its twin in the red clay or
the graceful scapulae   featherless wings of angels
or the perfect skulls
the size of my grandmother's porcelain teacups
that let morning sun shine through their fragile skins
it was not even the acrid scent of interrupted lives
clinging to my nostrils my clothes my fingertips

it was the first pocket in the worn cotton pants
laying flat on a wooden plank table in a field of yellow grass
holding a child-size handful of marbles
glass treasures   miniature globes of other little boy's worlds
boys who didn't have to give their childhoods or their lives
to be soldiers

later there was the saffron and scarlet pocket of the woman
filled with a mother's things
a rattle   a small wooden building block
with a faded blue giraffe an orange house
and a worn apple green letter "A" on the last side

"A" the first letter I learned   the beginning of story
disparate episodes told in an ivory calligraphy
of tibias of the angel wings of scapulae

full pockets hold real time
hold lives in front of the shadows left by bleached bones
in silent red earth below an unforgiving African sky

what we forget

we have been married to the earth our entire lives
scarlet sneakers caked with her mud
sun-warmed sand along the landscape of our backs
frozen toes from the turquoise of her glacial lakes
all around us now we see her letting go
feel the release of her embrace

we clasp her tightly along canal walks
during sunsets   we breathe the golden air of Israel
the magenta Pacific sky
the bronzed edge of a hundred lakes
we hurl ourselves through night
the birthing of wild stars
sapphire light splashed on denuded mountainsides
the dulled skin of dying fish gilding the stalks of rotted plants
we bleed ourselves into her dying rivers
that shone silver once in the milk of moonlight
we sing our own silence
listen to the stories she speaks in mountain stream and wind
in ocean wave and the whisper of fog
stories we must tell as we gather into new constellations
the cobalt words of now
of women dancing glowing—their breath a cloud of winter

messages

for this pocket of time
we glide into the center of glacial memory
slide within our cedar strip
become heart surrounded by this flesh of evergreens
that grows on the bones of pink granite
scraped smooth in the time before language
trees that scribe their rooted messages below our feet
lay their needles into a calligraphy on the forest floor
hieroglyphs of bronze that say
> *remember to smell our exhalation Christmas tree air*
> *listen for the chorus of loons who trill*
> *who echo darkness*
> > *they teach the purity of sound*
> *remember how the light at sunset gilds the forest floor*
> > *for the length of a breath*

if you wake in the center of a black velvet night
after the silken petals of the water lilies
close around themselves
the lake becomes glass
the moon shows her full countenance
behind a smear of opalescent cloud
you can taste everything

how to pick a raspberry

I
some people feel you must protect yourself
with long sleeves   long pants   and a wide brimmed hat
I don't
I walk in the fields bare-headed   no sleeves
soft canvas wrapped around my feet
with a few raggedy holes to let in summer rain

II
open your hand slowly
slide into the thorned community of bushes
the berries live here
a family below a canopy of emerald leaves
grasp each fruit gently   a raspberry bleeds easily
slide it off the knobby-cream penis it clings to
she will slide into your hand when she is ready
feel her skin
it is your skin
soft and warm from the sun
scarlet from her summer mornings
lay her gently into your basket
or open your mouth
lay her on your tongue
feel her juice in your mouth
her seeds beneath your teeth
she is gone in a moment

a question of loss
"What are we supposed to do with all this loss?"
Margaret Atwood

in early dawns
some women go to the rivers
they walk barefoot on damp earth
through the razors of nettles
to place their losses in lidded baskets
hidden by the emerald and sable curtains of cattails

other women
come outside of their pueblos to mix red and white clays
coil and smooth the clay into pots
fire the pots in square wombs
nesting in the fires they have built on the earth
they carve their losses on the skins of these pots
born of their fingers and their fires

some women
rip their clothes into rags until they are naked
weave their rags into baskets
into rugs that are soft and bright as their children
they entwine their losses in the spirals of their designs

some women
shear the wool from their sheep
dye it with onions   beets and wildflowers
spin the wool into yarns
stitch the yarns into the empty white squares of canvases
their losses are the patterns of their tapestries

other women
keep their losses in bread dough
in the borders of wedding ring quilts
in drawers near silk underwear
in cupboards under the sink near the red and white dish towels
their losses live in their wombs
in the scarlet lace within their ivory bones
the sacred places where silence sings

zoo sleep over
(for m)

I leave you on this silvery morning
below a fingernail moon
a slight smile in a dawn sky
I leave you   at a campsite overlooking a plain
empty of the dance of giraffes   the evening charge of rhinos
to write on these pages of my journal   damp with rose petals
and the violet fingerprints
scattered by the jacarandas in springtime

you sleep in a tent for the first time
to celebrate your seventy-five years
I am certain still you will always be here   each time I return
certain as my daughter is that she will see me so
she barely mumbles *good-bye* in her sleep language
as I slide her black sleeping bag down a few inches
to uncover her strawberry curls
and her alabaster face one last time
before I leave our tent

when I said goodbye to you last night
I heard that familiar break in your voice
that always comes with our partings
the same one mine has now when I leave my daughters
it wasn't until my plane lifted
out of the bowl of your airport that my eyes filled
stinging with longing for another hug
another late night giggle about a bat in capri pants
a silly phrase from our new made-up sign language
or a one-legged yoga posture
in front of an enormous mosaic Buddha
who gleams in your California sunlight
our together ends—three generations circle each other
ribbons around a maypole
shimmering   damp with parting tears
the braid of time   the fabric remaining

moving your soul

my soul sometimes forgets to stretch itself out to my fingertips
it ends somewhere between my elbow and my wrist

it's been that way lately
I notice it when I hug the three year olds
who populate my mornings
I notice it when I chop garlic into the confetti for scampi

I even noticed it once
when I lay next to you on a Saturday afternoon
during the sunlit hours where we create home
within the slumber of each other's arms

so I exercise
I eat more broccoli
I knit
I loop and slide ruby and lapis wool through my empty fingers
I let dark chocolate dissolve on my tongue
which doesn't fill my empty parts
but makes me smile

I go to see a thirteen month old I know
I inhale her milky baby scent
I say *bah bah* each time she says *bah*
I sing *Humpty Dumpty* as I bounce her on my knee
dip her as *Humpty* falls

then I find you   kiss your mouth
unbutton your flannel shirt one button at a time
pull each small ivory disc through its portal
until it separates   free on its own side
I breathe the scent of our long love
my soul moves toward my wrist--
along fingers into each whorl and line
my soulprint upon your skin   again

for these poets
(to linda and kathy)

we sit in the small turret of your kitchen
watch the lake reveal her spring jade skin
I see lives arc from the leaves of these poems
they rustle like taffeta below the late afternoon sky

Linda carries a thousand stories of her ancestors
paints aunts   grandmothers neighbors visible
they shine   behind their clotheslines   within their kitchens
into their time she threads the lives of far-away women
weaves all their lives into a glittering tapestry

Kathy carries creeks and rivers in her veins
we glide on her rafts of sound   laugh in her sunlit words
she threads us through her narrows
submerges us in the sorrow of her rapids
drenches us with her liquid truth

these pages   these bodies of words
from the hands of these women
stand open
sing the luminous danger of a woman's language
scream the fireworks of truth

the last poem

what place is this
where someone else decides
we must be protected from ourselves
we must be cleansed of the blood we come from
this world so far from our mothers
who gathered once in red tents to tell their stories
to live the importance of their lives together

we carry this life still
it flows   jewel scarlet   warm vermilion
it moves so generously
it is a field of wild poppies
whose enormous pleated faces open wide enough
to invite you within
it is the beds of the first tulips
that mirror our beauty in their petals

we must remember the old ways
remember to scatter ourselves
dance our way through fields in springtime
our flowerings on soft dark earth
this place where rubies fly
where one life nurtures another
where we walk arm in arm laughing
in celebration of the rose quartz of the young
the deep garnet   the incarnadine of now
and the night beauty of ancient red stars

Kathleen Shoemaker

For my children Dave, Jeff, Linda,
Tom, and Jim. And for Keith.

I have waited

For laundry to dry   babies to be born
Tomatoes to ripen   kids at the dentist
The moon to rise   my husband to come home
To finish school   be a good mother
For braces to come off   for a good marriage
To know myself   for spaghetti to cook
The sun to set   to use the bathroom
My marriage to end   new brakes on the car
For doctors to call   lovers to arrive
My son to die
Flowers to flower

The last time I walked in the rain

Cold washed over me
Soaked through the canvas
Of my light colored jacket
Dripped down behind my glasses
Followed the pull of gravity
Like tears I cried when I was married

Yanked like a hooked fish
From my summer world
A sandy-bottomed creek
Where I swam among the minnows
In and out dark forests of cattails
Leaping free mouth wide open
I savored split seconds of possibilities
When I made no one else's breakfast

"The roses have never been more beautiful."

Doesn't she know she said
Those very same words last year?
And the year before?
And the year before that?

Now I am the age my aunt was
When she wrote those words to me
And this year the roses
Have never been more beautiful.

Looking For The Om

Put on my hiking boots
Sturdy creviced soles that gripped
The sides of the Pyrenees in rain and sleet
Pulled me into the Kokonee Mountains
Alongside my sister
Who showed me where light
Sparkled among the trees
At the same time my son's body was cremated.

Into my worn and weathered backpack
Water stained with adventures
I layered ingredients for my urban hike
   black sweater, slacks, and fancy shoes
   turquoise necklace made by my friend
   who survived her own cross country hike
   from Auschwitz to Bergen-Belsen.

Hopped the el train at the airport
Went looking for the Om on the New York subway
Found him in the voice of a street person prophesying
   "Mother fuckers sending our kids to the killing fields"
In the mechanical incantations
   "This is the L train to Brooklyn. Next stop Grahame Avenue."
Heard him in the rattles, clanks, clatters of doors opening, shutting
Felt him in the hole in the New York skyline
Saw him in the woman digging in garbage
Next to a parked Rolls Royce
Felt his touch from Mahler's Tenth
Willie Nelson's offbeat rhythms
Footsteps pounding on the pavement
Saw him with pushcart vendors and their wares
In the turbulence of Times Square
Graffiti's urban sprawl
The drawings of a schizophrenic artist

I met him at a party
Drinking wine with other guests
He winked and shook my hand
Turned away to greet the others

When it came time came to leave the city
I put on my hiking boots
Sturdy creviced soles that had tramped
Across Manhattan
Glimpsed him from the taxi
As I journeyed in reverse

Homesick for the Om
I climbed the stairs up to my condo
Dumped my backpack on the bed
In the silence of the quiet
Unpacking memories of the city
I found him curled up on my sweater
Necklace in his hand

Yoga: Sweet Vampire
(For Francois)

Breathing down
Weaving consciousness
Into muscle and bone
I dive
Sip my own blood
I am
Replenished

Yoga Haiku

Reservoir of breath
Existential arrival
Homeostasis

Time Still

It surprises me now to hear the steps of my life following me."
                                            Galway Kinnell

I want time to spread out
Like icy film on the water
Clear and shiny
Reflect winter stars and shadows of trees
While naked breezes lift my eyelashes
And leave me wondering

I want time to calculate my life
To organize possessions
Neatly stack pale yellow sheets
Lace edged pillowcases
Deep blue Egyptian towels
To line drawers with red gingham shelf paper
Or patterns of daisies trailing ribbons
Algebraic formulas of precision
Each number and letter assigned a function
No room for different answers

I want time to build me a web
An elaborate construction
Where I stake out a three ring circus
Perform on a high wire of finest silk
Create new trajectories
Be my own side show
Prowl and swing
Devour mates
Rove perimeters I have staked out
Find my way to the center
Where I will find time still

This Normal Day

A walk around the lake with a friend—
Her middle daughter moved out over the weekend
Leaving the house sad

> *"It's time for her to go*
> *Our lives have been comfortably consistent*
> *My two daughters' and mine*
> *It's not like she moved to California or Germany*
> *She's just down the street*
> *We didn't know we would miss her so much"*

We stop between the currents of our conversation
Look at the branch of a pine tree
Reaching through clear air over autumn water
A few cones cling among the needles
Like baby possums to their mother's back

> *"My daughter wrote to me*
> *The one I haven't heard from for several months*
> *She's in the process of transgendering*
> *She was such a feminine little girl"*

Last week's storm did a lot of damage
We make our way around fallen branches
Skirt muddy places and puddles
Put down our footprints
We'll not get lost

trans (Latin, *beyond, through*)

Trans fats raise blood cholesterol levels
Increase one's risk of cardiovascular disease
The good news is that we can replace the body's store of them
With fish and olive oils

According to one expert
The world's supply of fish will be depleted by 2040
Another expert says that's hogwash
They did not mention anything about the world's supply of
  olives
On the same program I heard a dietician report
By changing her diet a few years ago
Her blood transmogrified from Western to Mediterranean

I think about my daughter who is transgendering
I would like to make it easy for him
No transplants to male heart or kidneys
But some potion that will gently
Soften the female deposits in her arteries
Loosen their grip to wend their way downstream
Until swirling eddies convince them to go otherwise

Then I would baptize her heart with good red wine—
He will feel strong reverberations of maleness
Echo through chambers
Celebrating this transatlantic voyage

The eye my son lost

When he was six years old
Plucked out by a surgeon
Replaced by an artist
Who knew how to craft eyes

The eye my son lost
Rolled under a dresser
Dust grew around it
While he wore a patch
But had no sword to defend himself

The eye my son lost
Didn't keep him from flying
He hired a lawyer
For a license to fly
And now he soars
A Cyclops a minotaur
My one-eyed son
The world in his eye

Interstices

First frost shimmering leaves
Light icing melting on your tongue
My mother's divinity
Puff balls of sweetened air
Midget clouds of sugar
Here and gone

A glacier calves
Shining blue-green shimmering child
Already melting cracks off and disappears
Drop by drop   no monumental melt down
No Witch of the North
No Chernobyl
Just slow silent dropping through my fingers
The ice cubes in my palms

I had a lover once
"*Chernobyl*" I whispered to him whenever he called
I stood in the corner far away as the phone would reach
Hiding from my boss
A cell phone would have solved the problem
But not the other problem – a persistent ache in residence
The doctor couldn't treat

A child of thirty bends over a container   it explodes
Tears his glasses from his face
He soars, a wingless dragon breathing fire
For a split second he must have thought
"*Look Mom, I can fly!*"
Before earth and time collided

Another glacier calves
The oldest child turns forty
A chunk of time implodes
Two ends collapse to meet themselves
Coming and going

Aunt Marie

Most of the time I knew my Aunt Marie
She was stout   ankles falling over
Her black old lady shoes
She wore her long gray hair in braids
Wrapped round her head like a tiara
Sometimes she let me sit on the back of the couch
Undo her braids and comb her hair down to her shoulders
I told her she looked like a queen

After dinner when the table was cleared
Down to the sheen of oilcloth
We'd sit in front of the fireplace
While she recited James Whitcomb Riley poems
The Raggedy Raggedy, Raggedy Man
Little Orphant Annie's Come To Our House To Stay

One other time I saw her with her hair down
She danced alone on the beach late at night
A glass of Scotch in her hand
The ice swirled as she moved
Feet bare skimming the sand
Moonlight on her hair
Shiny as silver filaments

Tin Types

I bought some old photographs
Tintypes from the flea market
Sober and serious Northern Europeans
Men in black hats with bearded faces
Women seated in stillness wearing dark dresses
Expressions holding back sorrow and laughter
A respectable family tree
Visual evidence that I came from somewhere

One grandfather embezzled money
Ran off to Canada with his family
Changed their name to MacEngelking
To disguise his German origins
They bought a wheat farm and built a new house
On the prairie a few miles from town
The house burned from being fumigated
My grandmother dead set against bugs and dirt
She was pregnant when another house burned
This time with two of their sons

The other grandfather's stroke
Reduced his reach and vocabulary.
Like a religious parrot all the feathers turned white
He repeated his mantra *"Jesus Christ, Jesus Christ"*
As though he could earn points in heaven

Once he was a millionaire
Owned a lumber mill and country store
Put on a tuxedo and went to the Governor's Ball.
According to Aunt Marie he was a womanizer
"Poor Ellie" she would say of his wife
Shake her head sorrow on her face and in her voice
I wonder if Ellie wanted to go to the Governor's Ball

Some photos are groups --- great, great aunts and uncles
Distant grandparents and cousins
Lives caught in one monochromatic act
Outside the photographs they gather for Sunday dinner
Exchange news   share companionship
The Canadian Rockies an apparition in the distance

A Ring My Mother Never Gave Me

She kept it in her bureau drawer
Wrapped in a handkerchief
Corners drawn together loosely
A nest of memories
Left-overs from the fire that ate up
Much of her mother's story
A grandmother I never knew
Because she died when I was a baby

My mother centered me carefully
On the white chenille bedspread
Helped me untie the knot
Fold back the embroidered corners
And play with pieces of jewelry from another time

I didn't know then the stories in the stones
Circled in rings of gold
Or the story clasped inside the locket
Pictures of two young boys
Who had died in the fire

My mother never wore the rings
Said opals were bad luck
The same kind of bad luck as birds
Flying into windows
"They both bring death" her mother told her

Years and years later another fire
Devoured much of my mother's history
She never wore the rings
But I do know she had seen
Birds fly into windows

Thistles
for Jo

We walked through the dry pasture
My father, older brother and I
Dad held my hand as we stepped around thistles
Spouting purple topknots like whales in far distant oceans

When I was older my dad
Paid my friend Jo and me
Fifty cents an hour to chop the thistles
Hoes in hand we lasted about an hour
In the summer heat and dust
Lied about how long we worked
Dropped our clothes
Locust shedding husks
To fall into the river's green silk

Scuffling along in white sneakers
Holding Dad's hand I stepped on a nail
We stopped --- the three of us a still life
My brother bent over wrapped his hands
Around my ankle unhooked me
Like the trout he caught in near-by streams

Sometimes we had those trout for breakfast
After my brother slit the white soft bellies
With his pocket knife and gutted them with his fingers
He swished them in a bucket of water
Blood stained the water circulating
They moved like they could swim again
Mom and Dad dipped them in cornmeal
To fry golden crisp in the electric frying pan
Taught us how to separate the halves
Peel out the skeleton

My white sneaker turned red
My father took me to the doctor
The needle for the tetanus shot got stuck
I wondered if I'd ever be able to go home

Ritual

Our small lives
Filled with abundance
Waking
Paper is here
Coffee is brewed
Toast is made
The pears are ripe
Ready for the mindful journey
From the kitchen
Through the living room
Down the hall
To our bedside table

I open the blinds
Morning comes by
Peeks in the windows
Decides to stay

Arranging ourselves
Side by side
Against piled up pillows
We click our cups in relief

Divergence

He tells me his life is diverging
Arcing away from the curve of common social history
Toward his cosmic journey
He tells me he doesn't need to pack

Before he leaves on a trip he always waters the plants
Closes the blinds along their tracks toward one another
They sway seductively then settle down
To keep the afternoon light from splashing
The mezzotints over our new couch

We bought the couch because the old one hurt our backs
We like to sit side by side before dinner
Over cups of ginger tea exchanging stories of our day
We reach across the afternoon to touch one another
Barely notice our hands and eyes
Continually search out the other's

He speaks about his coming journey as an adventure
Of his sadness that he can't take me with him
      "But I want to go with you—
      I would dress for a safari, for white water rafting
      Down the most dangerous rivers
      I would even go rock climbing
      And you know I'm afraid of heights."

He reminds me that he is not taking a suitcase
Asks would I always remember to water the plants
And to pull the blinds against the late afternoon sun

Living Space

The house is mine to keep
Three rooms besides the kitchen and the bath
Not much furniture
But filled with the lives
We've lived here together

Your grandmother's philodendron
Coils protectively around your history
Heartbeats peer from the pine basket
My daughter gave me
More curl under the sofa we chose together
To rest after a night of erratic skipping

Laughter smiles at us
From silver framed mirrors in the halls
Shines out from under lampshades
Bright as full spectrum light bulbs

Sadness lies folded in the drawer
Under the bed
Sighs
Turns over shifting quietly
Careful not to disturb

Conversations
Todays', yesterday's and the day's before
Murmur from the walls

"I'm sorry I'm old," he told me

As we drove the back roads of Vermont
I do notice our aging
More brown spots on our skin
More trips to the dermatologist
Sun screen, hats, vitamins
Preparations not so much to stop the advance
Nor to retrieve the irretrievable

We left her long ago
The seventeen year old
Wearing polka dot shorts
Standing on the roadside
Suitcase in hand
Filled with lotions, potions, magic
Undanced dances, unpainted pictures
Impossible possibilities
Carelessly packed

But to manage the slow departure of time
Leaking like the blood in your body
Levees weakening
No major storms or immediate devastation
An Alberta or a Katrina
But a continuous subtle inner erosion
Until colors appear
Spreading under your skin
"Like a bruised sunset," you say

Every day we patrol
Check for warning signs
Of what's down the road
Yield signs surely
And in the distance a stop sign

Recipe for Lies

Words suspended between moments
Gestate in the movement of breath
Rising gentle as a dreamy waltz
Until birthed and laid to rest
In their cradle's thin smile

Cover with a kitchen towel
Let rest for three days

On the third day they will have risen
Shining white as Wonder Bread
Nutrition questionable
Or turned heavy as eggless pancakes
Hard to chew as days' old bread

Serve to everyone

Vice Versa

The hurdy gurdy man dances
With his captive bear   ridiculous sight
A wild animal cavorting clumsily on hind legs
With a man who could be his dinner

Then there is his monkey on a leash
Dressed in bright red coat and hat
People clap as he holds out a cup
Like a monk begging for alms

Meanwhile the monk in the monkey's land
Has shed his clothes
Sleeps naked among the trees
Picks bugs from his matted hair

Role
for Kastle Brill

The mother goes to school and teaches biology
The girl goes to school and learns biology
The tortoise shell cat stays home incubating kittens
The mother uses the cat as an example of a sex-linked
   characteristic to her class

She hopes her daughter will be a scientist
The daughter wants her mother to let her have a dog
Not a tortoise shell cat that walks stiff-legged
   because the first owner was a vegetarian
   who fed the cat vegetables, mayonnaise
   and non-irradiated milk
Sometimes the girl walks stiff-legged to see what it
   would feel like to have rickets

The tortoise shell cat cries
Beginning delivery of another litter
The girl midwifes
She doesn't want the job but her mother
   wants her to know biology

Rickets cause a lot of birth problems
Eventually the cat died in childbirth
And was replaced by a canary

Traffic

Spring is too bright for me
Loudly intrudes
Thumping my interior
Like the car speaker next to me
Tulips and forsythia brazenly fluorescent
Jangle my nerves
Chartreuse hanging out on branches
Like kids on a street corner
Hormones surging
A tide of wild laughter
Creek overflowing reaching spreading
Touching the unknown
Geese pair up
Stretch long necks in warning

I want to stop Spring
Hold up my hand
A crossing guard in uniform
Stand in the middle of the street
Order flowers back under the earth
Halt sap from rising
Return the eggs to Mother Goose
Then when I'm ready
Beckon Spring forward

Humpty Dumpty Revisited

Humpty Dumpty fell off the wall
Onto the yellow brick road
Bounced gently a few times
Rolled back and forth sideways and oblong
Before uprighting to his feet
Looked down and saw his beaded moccasins were unscuffed
His short blue coat still neat and tidy
There were no scratches on his arms
No cracks in the long curve of his belly

He turned his head which was easier than he thought
Given that eggs don't have heads
Let his eyes follow the slope of his back
Searching for breaks or cracks
He realized he hadn't broken just felt a little scrambled
Like eggs one stirs together in the frying pan
And eats with buttered toast or buckwheat pancakes
The kind my father made for us on Sunday mornings
With hot chocolate made the way he liked it
Dark bitter and frothy
Sometimes we made him lemonade
Exactly to his specifications—
  juice of one lemon, a teaspoon of powdered sugar
  ice, water, a splash of grenadine

Humpty Dumpty was happy he hadn't broken
The ending was different now
He did wonder how the story would turn out

For Caroline and Margaret

"Let me carry it for you,"
Your box full of darkness

You don't have to tell me what's in it
Diamonds swimming in their own bright fires
Fireflies mating in the evening sky
Wild strawberries from the fields of your childhood
The unsaid

I'll carry this gift
The language of your poetry
Across the river in the moonlight
Through the meadow and into the forest

I know a place, a grove of ancient cedars
Where I will kneel in the soft green moss
Offer my breath as prayer
Wait for Night to come
And claim her own

Summer

I walk through summer
  to the pasture
  to sit among the horses
  and read poetry.

The river runs beside me, silent
  I take off my clothes
  slip under its cool sheen
  dream of a Prince.

I didn't know autumn would come so soon.

Poets' Biographies

Linda Drajem has taught for many years, first in Buffalo Public Schools and now at Buffalo State College. Despite a love of language and literature, she did not begin writing until later in life. As Anna Quindlen says there is great "power in the writing of ordinary people", which Linda has celebrated as a teacher and writer in the Women of the Crooked Circle. She lives with her husband, Bob, in Buffalo, but often travels to visit sons, their spouses, plus four precious grandchildren. She has been published in the *Buffalo News*, *Pure Light*, *Intuitions*.

Barbara Quirk Faust teaches and writes with the three, four, and five-year-olds at Bennett Park Montessori Center in Buffalo, New York. She is honored to be a writing member of the Women of the Crooked Circle. She facilitates writing groups for other teachers as well as in the community. Her poetry has been published in *Writers Who Cook*, the *Buffalo News* and *Reading Teacher*. She and her husband, Jerry, divide their time between a flat in Buffalo and a small hundred-year-old cottage in Toronto.

Kathleen Shoemaker wrote her first poems as an English class assignment in college. She took a break for many years while she raised a family, worked in the art and framing business, and became a certified yoga teacher. Her first experience with a writing group was in 1995 as a member of the HAGS in Spokane, Washington. When she moved to Buffalo in 1996, she joined the Women of the Crooked Circle. She and her husband Keith Elkins live in Buffalo, New York.

Printed in the United States
200235BV00003B/1-219/A